D1566007

The Bird / Poem Book

Books by Hayden Carruth

POETRY

The Crow and the Heart
Journey to a Known Place
The Norfolk Poems
North Winter
Nothing for Tigers
Contra Mortem
For You
The Clay Hill Anthology

FICTION

Appendix A

CRITICISM

After the Stranger: Imaginary Dialogues with Camus

ANTHOLOGIES

The Voice That Is Great Within Us
The Bird/Poem Book

THE
BIRD/ POEM
BOOK

Poems on the Wild Birds of North America

Selected by

HAYDEN CARRUTH

With illustrations by Mel Hunter

The McCall Publishing Company
New York

Published simultaneously in Canada by
Doubleday Canada Ltd., Toronto

Library of Congress Catalog Card Number: 73-122118

SBN 8415-0043-6

Printed in the United States of America

Design by Tere LoPrete

Acknowledgments

The following poems in this anthology are reproduced by permission of the authors, their publishers, or their agents:

"How Many Nights" from *Body Rags*, by Galway Kinnell, copyright © 1965, 1967 by Galway Kinnell. Reprinted by permission of the publisher, Houghton Mifflin Company.

"Sparrow" from *The Broken Ground*, by Wendell Berry, copyright © 1964 by Wendell Berry. Reprinted by permission of Harcourt Brace Jovanovich, Inc.

"Birds" from *The Selected Poetry of Robinson Jeffers*, copyright © 1925 and renewed 1953 by Robinson Jeffers. Reprinted by permission of Random House, Inc.

"Birds Waking" from *Green With Beasts*, by W.S. Merwin. Published 1956 by Alfred A. Knopf, Inc. Reprinted by permission of the publisher and of David Higham Associates, Ltd.

"A Canticle to the Waterbirds" from *The Crooked Lines of God*, by Brother Antoninus. Copyright © 1960 by University of Detroit Press. Reprinted by permission of publisher.

"Swallows" from *Words for Denver and Other Poems*, by Thomas Hornsby Ferril. Copyright © 1952, 1954, 1957, 1960, 1963, 1966 by Thomas Hornsby Ferril. Reprinted by permission of Willian Morrow & Company, Inc.

"The Osprey's Nest" from *Staying Alive*, by David Wagoner. Copyright © 1966 by Indiana University Press. Reprinted by permission of Indiana University Press.

"The Distances They Keep" from *The Blue Swallows*, by Howard Nemerov, copyright © 1967 by Howard Nemerov.

"Claritas" from *O Taste and See*, by Denise Levertov, copyright © 1964 by Denise Levertov Goodman; "The Irate Songster" from *Collected Poems*, by Kenneth Patchen, copyright © 1952 by Kenneth Patchen; "GIC to HAR" from *Collected Shorter Poems*, by Kenneth Rexroth, copyright ©

Foreword

People who consult field guides and manuals in their study of wild birds are often disappointed. The descriptions seem clumsy or vague; sometimes they simply don't say what the bird looks like—in two hundred studiously chosen words. Photographs may help, and drawings, especially silhouettes, may help even more; but this is a paradox. Why should we come closer to the bird itself as we abandon objective description and move toward subjective impressionism? Is it because the bird, considered as an object of this world, is such a complex union of attributes that to describe it in words, to describe it objectively, precisely, completely, and recognizably, is well-nigh impossible? I think so. Better by far to catch the bird's characteristic stance or outline, its motion or look or mannerism—in short, its fleeting essence—and for this, the techniques of art are more useful than those of analysis and description.

If this is true of graphic art, it is equally true of poetry. Not one of our modern American poets, as far as I know, is a trained ornithologist. Yet many are such marvelous observers, and so skillful with language and imagery, that they can capture, often in few words, the intrinsic qualities of the birds with an aptness that makes them come alive to us. We know them—we *identify* them. This is one of the pleasures of birdwatching in the field. We all like to know what bird we are looking at, and some of us keep lists of species we have identified. What could be more gratifying, or more simple and human? But this same pleasure—in identification or what poets call recognition—is an element of poetry-reading too; and in both cases, birdwatching and poetry-reading, it leads on to other pleasures more profound and meaningful.

Significantly, nature poetry in this sense is recent. Most famous birds of literature—Keats' nightingale, Wordsworth's cuckoo, Shelley's skylark, Bryant's waterfowl, or hundreds of others—are not present to our sight at all. The poets failed to say what they look like. We wouldn't know their species if they weren't named in the titles of the poems, and to this day we can't tell if Bryant's waterfowl was a bittern or a wood duck or, for that matter, a flamingo. The poets were preoccupied with their own feelings, and used the birds merely as pegs on which to hang their own joys and sorrows. We must go back to Chaucer, to the medieval world of hieratic order, before we come to the idea that birds are worth writing about for their own sake, or for God's sake. In our time poets have begun to regain this respect for the objects of the nonhuman world. They believe (as did a few of their forerunners, those poets of the past who have a particular influence on modern practice) that a bird has as much claim to actuality as anyone or anything else. Hence, if they write a bird poem they know that whatever else they put into it they must give first place to the bird, whole and alive, an identifiable selfhood.

Is this new respect for birds, almost reverence for them, a function of the poet's awareness that their existence has become suddenly tenuous and fragile? Are the birds slipping from us, so that we reach out to hold them, in our poems as in our sanctuaries? I don't know. Other reasons, drawn from the technical evolution of poetry, may account for the changed attitudes of poets. But the world is changing too, the natural environment on which mankind has always relied for cultural as well as material support; it is changing very, very fast; and poets aren't alone in learning how precious its natural objects are as they—the objects and perhaps the poets—pause on the edge of extinction.

At all events here are a few real birds living in the minds of men. The drawings by Mel Hunter combine a naturalist's knowledge and experience with an artist's imagination, and so give us images that are, in their pictorial realm, genuine insights. The poems have been written by many poets, young and old, living and dead, famous and obscure. All the poems are modern except for two, which are modern in spirit, and all the birds specified in the poems are common to North America. Finally it seems to me that each of these works, verbal and visual, brings us the kind of sudden sweet perception that makes life in nature a meaningful human experience, just as each was certainly done in the kind of attention, knowledge, and intelligence that we call love.

H. C.

Contents

The Bird / Poem Book

ROBERT   FRANCIS

The Seed Eaters

The seed eaters, the vegetarian birds,
Redpolls, grosbeaks, crossbills, finches, siskins,
Fly south to winter in our north, so making
A sort of Florida of our best blizzards.

Weed seeds and seeds of pine cones are their pillage.
Alder and birch catkins, such vegetable
Odds and ends as the winged keys of maple
As well as roadside sumac, red-plush-seeded.

Hi! with a bounce in snowflake flocks come juncos
As if a hand had flipped them and tree sparrows,
Now nip and tuck and playing tag, now squatting
All weather-proofed and feather-puffed on snow.

Hard fare, full feast, I'll say, deep cold, high spirits.
Here's Christmas to Candlemas on a bunting's budget.
From this old seed eater with his beans, his soybeans,
Cracked corn, cracked wheat, peanuts and split peas, hail!

MICHAEL   ONDAATJE

Description Is a Bird

In the afternoon while the sun twists down
they come piggle piggle piggle all around the air.
Under clouds of horses the sand swallows turn

quick and gentle as wind.
All virtuoso performances
that presume a magnificent audience.

Skating on wings
their tails sensitive rudders,
the leader flings his neck back,
turns thinner than whims.
Like God the others follow
anticipating every twist,
the betrayals of a feather.

For them no thumping wing beat of a crow,
they bounce on a breath
like stones on water
scattering with the discipline of a watch.

DAVID   WAGONER

The Osprey's Nest

The osprey's nest has dropped of its own weight
After years, breaking everything under it, collapsing
Out of the sky like the wreckage of the moon,
Having killed its branch and rotted its lodgepole:
A flying cloud of fishbones tall as a man,
A shambles of dead storms ten feet across.

Uncertain what holds anything together,
Ospreys try everything—fishnets and broomsticks,
Welcome-mats and pieces of scarecrows,
Sheep bones, shells, the folded wings of mallards—
And heap up generations till they topple.

In the nest the young ones, calling fish to fly
Over the water toward them in old talons,
Thought only of hunger diving down their throats
To the heart, not letting go—(not letting go,
Ospreys have washed ashore, ruffled and calm
But drowned, their claws embedded in salmon).
They saw the world was bones and curtain-rods,
Hay-wire and cornstalks—rubble put to bed
And glued into meaning by large appetites.
Living on top of everything that mattered,
The fledglings held it in the air with their eyes,
With awkward claws groping the ghosts of fish.

Last night they slapped themselves into the wind
And cried across the rain, flopping for comfort
Against the nearest branches, baffled by leaves
And the blank darkness falling below their breasts.
Where have they gone? The nest, now heaped on the bank,
Has come to earth smelling as high as heaven.

10

BROTHER ANTONINUS

A Canticle to the Waterbirds

Written for the Feast of Saint Francis of Assisi, 1950

Clack your beaks you cormorants and kittiwakes,
North on those rock-croppings finger-jutted into the rough Pacific
surge;
You migratory terns and pipers who leave but the temporal
clawtrack written on sandbars there of your presence;
Grebes and pelicans; you comber-picking scoters and you
shorelong gulls;
All you keepers of the coastline north of here to the Mendocino
beaches;
All you beyond upon the cliff-face thwarting the surf at Hecate
Head;
Hovering the under-surge where the cold Columbia grapples at
the bar;
North yet to the Sound, whose islands float like a sown flurry of
chips upon the sea:
Break wide your harsh and salt-encrusted beaks unmade for song
And say a praise up to the Lord.

And you freshwater egrets east in the flooded marshlands skirting
the sea-level rivers, white one-legged watchers of shallows;
Broad-headed kingfishers minnow-hunting from willow stems on
meandering valley sloughs;
You too, you herons, blue and supple-throated, stately, taking the
air majestical in the sunflooded San Joaquin,

Grading down on your belted wings from the upper lights of
  sunset,
Mating over the willow clumps or where the flatwater rice fields
  shimmer;
You killdeer, high night-criers, far in the moon-suffusion sky;
Bitterns, sand-waders, all shore-walkers, all roost-keepers,
Populates of the 'dobe cliffs of the Sacramento:
Open your water-dartling beaks,
And make a praise up to the Lord.

For you hold the heart of His mighty fastnesses,
And shape the life of His indeterminate realms.
You are everywhere on the lonesome shores of His wide creation.
You keep seclusion where no man may go, giving Him praise;
Nor may a woman come to lift like your cleaving flight her clear
  contralto song
To honor the spindrift gifts of His soft abundance.
You sanctify His hermitage rocks where no holy priest may kneel
  to adore, nor holy nun assist;
And where his true communion-keepers are not enabled to enter.

And well may you say His praises, birds, for your ways
Are verved with the secret skills of His inclinations,
And your habits plaited and rare with the subdued elaboration of
  His intricate craft;
Your days intent with the direct astuteness needful of His infinite
  sleep.
You are His secretive charges and you serve His secretive ends,
In His clouded mist-conditioned stations, in His murk,
Obscure in your matted nestings, immured in His limitless ranges.
He makes you penetrate through dark interstitial joinings of His
  thicketed kingdoms,
And keep your concourse in the deeps of His shadowed world.

Your ways are wild but earnest, your manners grave,
Your customs carefully schooled to the note of His serious mien.
You hold the prime condition of His clean creating,
And the swift compliance with which you serve His minor means
Speaks of the constancy with which you hold Him.
For what is your high flight forever going home to your first
    beginnings,
But such a testament to your devotion?
You hold His outstretched world beneath your wings, and mount
    upon His storms,
And keep your sheer wind-lidded sight upon the vast perspectives
    of His mazy latitudes.

But mostly it is your way that you bear existence wholly within
    the context of His utter will and are untroubled.
Day upon day you do not reckon, nor scrutinize tomorrow, nor
    multiply the nightfalls with a rash concern,
But rather assume each instant as warrant sufficient of His final
    seal.
Wholly in Providence you spring, and when you die you look on
    death in clarity unflinched,
Go down, a clutch of feather ragged upon the brush;
Or drop on water where you briefly lived, found food,
And now yourselves make food for His deep current-keeping fish,
    and then are gone:
Is left but the pinion-feather spinning a bit on the uproil
Where lately the dorsal cut clear air.

You leave a silence. And this for you suffices, who are not of the
    ceremonials of man,
And hence are not made sad to now forgo them.
Yours is of another order of being, and wholly it compels.
But may you, birds, utterly seized in God's supremacy,
Austerely living under his austere eye—

Yet may you teach a man a necessary thing to know,
Which has to do of the strict conformity that creaturehood
    entails,
And constitutes the prime commitment all things share.
For God has given you the imponderable grace to *be* His
    verification,
Outside the mulled incertitude of our forensic choices;
That you, our lessers in the rich hegemony of Being,
May serve as testament to what a creature is,
And what creation owes.

Curlews, stilts and scissortails, beachcomber gulls,
Wave-haunters, shore-keepers, rockhead-holders, all cape-top
    vigilantes,
Now give God praise.
Send up the strict articulation of your throats,
And say His name.

Goldfinches

The hayfield is not afire,
Yet sparks fly upward.
Crisscross then, and looping,
They dive down backward.

Pigeon

This bird is used to sitting on bright ledges
And looking into darkness. Through the square
High window in the barn the mow is black
To one here by the fence. But there he sits
And treads the sun-warm sill, turning his breast
Toward all the musty corners deep within.
They flash no colors on him, though the sky
Is playing bronze and green upon his back.
Gravely he disappears, and spiders now
Must hurry from the rafter where his beak
Searches the seed. The afternoon is slow
Till he returns, complacent on the ledge,
And spreads a breast of copper. But the sun
Is nothing to a pigeon. On the ground
A grain of corn is yellower than gold.
He circles down and takes it, leisurely.

Humming-Bird

I can imagine, in some otherworld
Primeval-dumb, far back
In that most awful stillness that only gasped and hummed,
Humming-birds raced down the avenues.

Before anything had a soul,
While life was a heave of Matter, half inanimate,
This little bit chipped off in brilliance
And went whizzing through the slow, vast, succulent stems.

I believe there were no flowers then,
In the world where the humming-bird flashed ahead of creation.
I believe he pierced the slow vegetable veins with his long beak.

Probably he was big
As mosses and little lizards, they say, were once big.
Probably he was a jabbing, terrifying monster.

We look at him through the wrong end of the telescope of Time,
Luckily for us.

Swallows

The prairie wind blew harder than it could,
Even the spines of cactus trembled back,
I crouched in an arroyo clamping my hands
On my eyes the sand was stinging yellow black.

In a break of the black I let my lashes part,
Looked overhead and saw I was not alone,
I could almost reach through the roar and almost touch
A treadmill of swallows almost holding their own.

Birds Waking

I went out at daybreak and stood on Primrose Hill.
It was April: a white haze over the hills of Surrey
Over the green haze of the hills above the dark green
Of the park trees, and over it all the light came up clear,
The sky like deep porcelain paling and paling,
With everywhere under it the faces of the buildings
Where the city slept, gleaming white and quiet,
St. Paul's and the water tower taking the gentle gold.
And from the hill chestnuts and the park trees
There was such a clamor rose as the birds woke,
Such uncontainable tempest of whirled
Singing flung upward and upward into the new light,
Increasing still as the birds themselves rose
From the black trees and whirled in a rising cloud,
Flakes and water-spouts and hurled seas and continents of them
Rising, dissolving, streamering out, always
Louder and louder singing, shrieking, laughing.
Sometimes one would break from the cloud but from the song
    never,
And would beat past my ear dinning his deafening note.
I thought I had never known the wind
Of joy to be so shrill, so unanswerable,
With such clouds of winged song at its disposal, and I thought
Oh Voice that my demand is the newest name for,
There are many ways we may end, and one we must,
Whether burning, or the utter cold descending in darkness,
Explosion of our own devising, collision of planets, all
Violent, however silent they at last may seem;
Oh let it be by this violence, then, let it be now.

Now when in their sleep, unhearing, unknowing,
Most faces must be closest to innocence,
When the light moves unhesitating to fill the sky with clearness
And no dissent could be heard above the din of its welcome,
Let the great globe well up and dissolve like its last birds,
With the bursting roar and uprush of song!

GIC to HAR

It is late at night, cold and damp,
The air is filled with tobacco smoke.
My brain is worried and tired.
I pick up the encyclopedia,
The volume GIC to HAR,
It seems I have read everything in it,
So many other nights like this.
I sit staring empty-headed at the article "Grosbeak,"
Listening to the long rattle and pound
Of freight cars and switch engines in the distance.
Suddenly I remember
Coming home from swimming
In Ten Mile Creek,
Over the long moraine in the early summer evening,
My hair wet, smelling of waterweeds and mud.
I remember a sycamore in front of a ruined farmhouse,
And instantly and clearly the revelation
Of a song of incredible purity and joy,
My first rose-breasted grosbeak,
Facing the low sun, his body
Suffused with light.
I was motionless and cold in the hot evening
Until he flew away, and I went on, knowing
In my twelfth year one of the great things
Of my life had happened.
Thirty factories empty their refuse in the creek.
The farm has given way to an impoverished suburb,

On the parched lawns are starlings, alien and aggressive.
And I am on the other side of the continent
Ten years in an unfriendly city.

Sparrow

A sparrow is
his hunger organized.
Filled, he flies
before he knows he's going to.
And he dies by the
same movement: filled
with himself, he goes
by the eye-quick
reflex of his flesh
out of sight,
leaving his perfect
absence without a thought.

DENISE LEVERTOV

Claritas

I

The All-Day Bird, the artist,
whitethroated sparrow,
striving
in hope and
good faith to make his notes
ever more precise, closer
to what he knows.

II

There is the proposition
and the development.
The way
one grows from the other.
The All-Day Bird
ponders.

III

May the first note
be round enough
and those that follow
fine, fine as
sweetgrass,

       prays
the All-Day Bird.

IV

Fine
as the tail of a lizard,
as a leaf of
chives—
the *shadow of a difference*
falling between
note and note,
a *hair's breadth*
defining them.

V

The dew is on the vineleaves.
My tree
is lit with the
break of day.

VI

Sun
light.
    Light
light light light.

ROBINSON JEFFERS

Birds

The fierce musical cries of a couple of sparrowhawks hunting
    on the headland,
Hovering and darting, their heads northwestward,
Prick like silver arrows shot through a curtain the noise of the
    ocean
Trampling its granite; their red backs gleam
Under my window around the stone corners; nothing gracefuller,
    nothing
Nimbler in the wind. Westward the wave-gleaners,
The old gray sea-going gulls are gathered together, the northwest
    wind wakening
Their wings to the wild spirals of the wind-dance.
Fresh as the air, salt as the foam, play birds in the bright wind,
    fly falcons
Forgetting the oak and the pinewood, come gulls
From the Carmel sands and the sands at the river-mouth, from
    Lobos and out of the limitless
Power of the mass of the sea, for a poem
Needs multitude, multitudes of thoughts, all fierce, all flesh-eaters,
    musically clamorous
Bright hawks that hover and dart headlong, and ungainly
Gray hungers fledged with desire of transgression, salt slimed
    beaks, from the sharp
Rock-shores of the world and the secret waters.

October Textures

The brushy and hairy,
tassely and slippery

willow, fragmitie,
cattail, goldenrod.

The fluttery, whistley
water-dimpling divers,

waders, shovelers,
coots and rocking scaup.

Big blue, little green,
horned grebe, godwit,

bufflehead, ruddy,
marsh hawk, clapper rail.

Striated water
and striated feather.

The breast of the sunset.
The phalarope's breast.

Pigeons

Wherever I go to find
peace or an island
under palms in the afternoon
at midnight to pity my neighborhood
at dawn in the shrubs
to look for a child

I hear them
they fly by
applauding themselves
I see them
they pray as they walk
their eyes are halos
around a pit
they look amazed

Who are these that come
as a cloud to our windows
who rush up like smoke
before the town burns

You will find one
on a mountain
in a carpenter's shop
at home on the lawn
of an old estate
at the library
in the forehead of paradise

Whoever is mad
can accuse them
thousands were killed in a day

What happens to them
happens to me
when I can't sleep
they moan and I'm there
and it's still like that

the head gone,
      the black escutcheon of the breast
            undecipherable,
an effigy of a sparrow,
      a dried wafer only,
            left to say
and it says it
      without offense,
            beautifully;
This was I,
      a sparrow.
            I did my best;
farewell.

The Distances They Keep

They are with us always, but they have the wit
To stay away. We are walking through the woods,
A sudden bush explodes into sparrows, they
Show no desire to become our friends.
So also with the pheasant underfoot
In the stubble field; and lazy lapwings rise
To give their slow, unanimous consent
They want no part of us, who dare not say,
Considering the feathers in our caps,
They are mistaken in the distances they keep.

Still, the heart goes out to them. Goes out,
But maybe it's better this way. Let them stay
Pieces of world we're not responsible for,
Who can be killed by cleverness and hate,
But, being shy enough, may yet survive our love.

Winter in Vermont

1.

Five
jays
discuss
goodandevil
in a
white
birch

like five
blue
fingers
playing
a
guitar.

2.

Snow buntings whirling
on a snowy field—
cutglass reflections
on a ceiling.

3.

Lover of balsam and lover of white pine
o crossbill crossbill
cracking unseen with of all things scissors
seeds seeds
a fidget for ears enpomped in the meadow's
silence silence
a crackling thorn aflame in the meadow's
cold cold.

4.
Small things
    are hardest to believe:
a redpoll snatching
    drops from an icicle.

    5.
The song of the gray
ninepointed buck
contains much contains
the whole north for
example the sweet
sharp whistling of
the redpolls caught
overhead in the branches
of the yellow birch
like leaves left over
from autumn and at
night the remote
chiming of stars
caught in the tines
of his quiet exaltation.

The Irate Songster

I went into my parlor
Sang the sparrow bird
There sat policeman
I busta yohs head see
I grinda yohs feets
Lika dem wormz
Yohs no minda m'biz take thet
Yohs bigga loafeh yohs
Phooeyz blooeyz blahz on yohs
I squeeza yohs noz
I teara
Yohs eyez off'r yohs faz
Ptooeyz
Take thet yohs ret
Thisa my own house see
No policeman
Sitz in my parlor

Onless I want 'm to

GALWAY KINNELL

How Many Nights

How many nights
have I lain in terror,
O Creator Spirit, Maker of night and day,

only to walk out
the next morning over the frozen world
hearing under the creaking of snow
faint, peaceful breaths . . .
snake,
bear, earthworm, ant . . .

and above me
a wild crow crying '*yaw yaw yaw*'
from a branch nothing cried from ever in my life.

Song for a Summer Afternoon

I look from my cage of cold
that hums like some sleepy monster
at the green trees waving over the tumble-down garage.
And the mourning dove mourns with the name of my long-lost
love.

I hear the sparrows snipping pieces out of the hush,
I hear the cicadas murmur, voice of the silence,
of loneliness, invisible thread binding the years together.
And the mourning dove mourns with the name of my long-lost
love.

I hear upon the thresholds of their cloudy kennels
the dogs of the thunder growling deep in their throats
as they strain at the yellow leashes of lightning.
And the mourning dove mourns with the name of my long-lost
love.

All the summer days are one day, sick-sweet with the jasmine of
yearning,
and I have grown neither taller nor older,
but only my shadow.
And the mourning dove mourns with the name of my long-lost
love.

Skimmers

Where you see the undersides of their wings
the whole mass is white and flickering in the sunlight
above the sandbar and the blue water of the sound
and you can hear them crying and protesting
in the cool sea wind that blows across the channel

and where the rest of them are turning toward you
they are all black and flickering in the sunlight
and they go swinging in a long Cartesian figure
like a twisted plane that lets you see its outlines
by its colors, the one half white and tilting away,

and the other half black and tilting toward you,
as they swing into the air and call you all the names
they can think of in the time it takes to rise
and get away, loping on their long black wings
so leisurely toward the sound behind the islands.

THEODORE ROETHKE

All Morning

Here in our aging district the wood pigeon lives with us,
His deep-throated cooing part of the early morning,
Far away, close-at-hand, his call floating over the on-coming
    traffic,
The lugubriously beautiful plaint uttered at regular intervals,
A protest from the past, a reminder.

They sit, three or four, high in the fir-trees back of the house,
Flapping away heavily when a car blasts too close,
And one drops down to the garden, the high rhododendron,
Only to fly over to his favorite perch, the cross-bar of a telephone
    pole;
Grave, hieratic, a piece of Assyrian sculpture,
A thing carved of stone or wood, with the dull iridescence of
    long-polished wood,
Looking at you without turning his small head,
With a round vireo's eye, quiet and contained,
Part of the landscape.

And the Steller jay, raucous, sooty headed, lives with us,
Conducting his long wars with the neighborhood cats,
All during mating season,
Making a racket to wake the dead,
To distract attention from the short-tailed ridiculous young ones
Hiding deep in the blackberry bushes—
What a scuttling and rapping along the drainpipes,
A fury of jays, diving and squawking,
When our spayed female cat yawns and stretches out in the
    sunshine—
And the wrens scold, and the chickadees frisk and frolic,

48

Pitching lightly over the high hedgerows, dee-deeing,
And the ducks near Lake Washington waddle down the highway
    after a rain,
Stopping traffic, indignant as addled old ladies,
Pecking at crusts and peanuts, their green necks glittering;
And the hummingbird dips in and around the quince tree,
Veering close to my head,
Then whirring off sideways to the top of the hawthorn,
Its almost-invisible wings, buzzing, hitting the loose leaves
    intermittently—

A delirium of birds!
Peripheral dippers come to rest on the short grass,
Their heads jod-jodding like pigeons;
The gulls, the gulls far from their waves
Rising, wheeling away with harsh cries,
Coming down on a patch of lawn:

It is neither spring nor summer: it is Always,
With towhees, finches, chickadees, California quail, wood doves,
With wrens, sparrows, juncos, cedar waxwings, flickers,
With Baltimore orioles, Michigan bobolinks,
And those birds forever dead,
The passenger pigeon, the great auk, the Carolina paraquet,
All birds remembered, O never forgotten!
All in my yard, of a perpetual Sunday,
All morning! All morning!

GEORGE HITCHCOCK

May All Earth Be Clothed In Light

Morning spreads over
the beaches like lava;
the waves lie still, they
glitter with pieces of light.

I stand at the window
& watch a heron on one leg,
its plumage white in the green banks
of mint. Behind me
smoke rises from its nest
of bricks, the brass clock
on the kitchen shelf
judges & spares.

Slowly the bird
opens its dazzling wings.
I am filled with joy.
The fields are awake!
the fields with their hidden lizards
& fire of new iris.